Saint Patrick

The Irish Saint

by Ruth Roquitte

Illustrated by Robert Kilbride

Dillon Press, Inc.   Minneapolis, Minnesota 55415

Library of Congress Cataloging in Publication Data

Roquitte, Ruth.
   Saint Patrick, the Irish Saint.

   SUMMARY: An easy-to-read biography of Ireland's patron
saint.
   1. Patrick, Saint, 373?-463?—Juvenile literature. 2. Christian saints—Ireland—Biography—Juvenile literature.
[1. Patrick, Saint, 373?-463? 2. Saints] I. Kilbride, Robert.
II. Title.
BR1720.P26R66   270.2'092'4 [B] [92]   81-3152

ISBN 0-87518-218-6   AACR2

Dillon Press, Inc., 500 South Third Street
Minneapolis, Minnesota 55415

Printed in the United States of America

Saint Patrick, the patron saint of Ireland, was born in Britain sometime around the year A.D. 385. He was a Roman citizen and a Christian. After Roman troops left Britain to fight in what now is France, he was captured by Irish raiders and sold as a slave. He spent six years in Ireland before his escape. It was during his years in slavery that Saint Patrick's faith in God grew strong. After a time of religious study, he returned to Ireland as a missionary and lived there until his death on March 17, 461. Under his leadership churches and schools were built, and Ireland became a center for Christian learning.

A Day in Springtime

There's a day in the spring when people wear green. It may be snowing in Alaska, or a sunny, hot day in Arizona. But on that day, it's springtime in Ireland. On that day almost all of us would like to be Irish.

Shamrocks and green hats appear in stores and in schoolrooms. In New York City, there's a big parade, as there has been on this day since 1762. As you may have guessed, we are talking about Saint Patrick's Day. This holiday is celebrated each year on March 17.

In Ireland, March 17 is a national holiday. No one goes to work or to school. Saint Patrick's

Day is also a holy day. People go to church and sing,

All praise to Saint Patrick
Who brought to our mountains
The gift of God's faith,
The sweet light of his love!

Who was the man we call Saint Patrick? Why do people honor him each year?

The story of Saint Patrick took place a long, long time ago. Our land was unknown to the people of Europe. The European nations of today did not exist. The Romans ruled most of Europe, and Roman soldiers kept order there and in the British Isles, too. The soldiers were followed by priests who carried the Christian faith to all parts of the Roman Empire.

This was the world Patrick was born in. His full name was Magonus Sucatus Patricius, and he was a free-born Roman citizen. His family was well to do. They owned land and had noble rank. His father was in the government, and he was also a deacon in the church. In that time

priests could marry and have children. Patrick's grandfather was a priest of the church.

This is about all we know. The only things we still have that Saint Patrick wrote are his "Confession" and one letter. In them, he tells us little about his early life. He does not even give the year of his birth. It is believed that he was born around A.D. 385. His place of birth was in Britain on a farm somewhere near the Irish Sea.

Saint Patrick does tell us that he was a spoiled boy. He preferred play to school. He did not listen to what his parents said. He paid little attention to his church lessons. In his "Confession," which he wrote many years later, Saint Patrick says that he was like a stone stuck in the mud. "I did not know the true God," he admits. All he thought about was having fun. His parents were afraid that he would come to no good.

Nobles like Patrick's family had a good life. Their homes were heated, had glass windows, and baths with hot and cold running water. Woolen clothes kept them warm. Fine foods filled their tables. On land they traveled by horse and chariot. On the sea sturdy sailing boats were used.

Patrick grew up with the sea and boats and, maybe, a thought or two of Ireland. That was the island that lay across the sea from where he lived. Not much was known about the people who lived there. They spoke their own language. Few of them spoke Latin, the language of the Romans. They had little to do with the people in Britain or Europe. For the most part, they stayed on their own little island.

Except the raiders. People who lived along the coast of Britain knew and feared the Irish raiders. Big, strong, fearless men, they robbed farms and villages and took captives. The people they took were doomed to become slaves of the Irish.

Roman soldiers in Britain had built forts along the sea to keep the Irish from slipping

past. Patrick may have watched as Roman soldiers marched over the roads. For many years they had kept Britain safe and made it a place of peace. Then they were called away to war. The forts that guarded the coast were empty.

After the soldiers left, Irish war trumpets were heard in Britain once more. And so it happened that Patrick first met the Irish one summer night.

(note that this was also the time of the Anglo Saxon invaders.)

Slave in Ireland

Patrick loved the farm where he had been born. The Irish Sea was nearby, and the shore was a fine place to explore. Servants took care of all his needs. It was peaceful and lovely. What more could a young boy want?

Did we say peaceful? How wrong we were. For one night, when Patrick was sixteen years old, that peace was broken.

The sea was calm and still that night. The moon was bright, and stars twinkled in the dark sky. Even the fast-moving boats speeding toward the shore did not break the silence. Thus the raiders easily slipped in from the sea. No

one knew. No one gave a warning.

Suddenly they blew their war trumpets! The noise woke all, both young and old. The blasts sent shivers of fear through everyone. "Raiders!" they cried.

It was too late! Patrick ran but could not escape. He fought with all his strength. Those big, strong men were too much for him. They tied him up and threw him in a boat.

Quickly the raiders worked. The old they killed. The small children they left alone. They captured the young and strong. They stole everything they could from the homes. The pirates worked by the light of the farms they set on fire. By sunrise they had set out to sea. No one could catch them now. Along with many other captives, they carried the boy who was to bring great change to their land.

Broken and bleeding, Patrick lay in the bottom of a boat. He was tied up hand and foot. Poor Patrick! He was lonely, afraid, hungry, and cold. What kind of life lay before him now?

The pirates sailed into an Irish port to sell their captives. The slave market was a busy place as buyers and sellers met. Patrick was bought by a man named Miliucc and taken to Mount Slemish. For six long years he worked in Ireland as a shepherd. The free-born noble boy was now a slave.

Patrick felt very much alone in that strange land. He tried to remember the Christian faith he had been taught. He prayed. He fasted. He thought constantly about God. As he tended sheep each day, he tells us, "Many times a day I prayed. The love of God and His fear came to me more and more, and my faith was strengthened."

In a single day, he prayed a hundred prayers and a hundred more at night. Yes, Patrick turned to God, and God gave him comfort.

The Escape

Patrick missed his family very much. He was homesick. Still, he worked hard and put his trust in God. Such faith did not go unnoticed. "And there one night," he writes, "I heard in my sleep a voice saying to me, 'It is well that you fast, soon you will go to your own country.' And again, after a short while, I heard a voice saying to me, 'See, your ship is ready.' "

That ship was far away, about two hundred miles. The place was unknown to Patrick. He had no friends there. Yet Patrick fled. God guided his path through forests and bogs. Danger lay all around, but no man or beast

Compare to Caedmon

19

could stop him. He reached the seaport and the waiting boat.

Patrick went to the captain. He told him that he could pay his way. The captain said that it was no use for him to ask to go along. Patrick was a stranger. He was a Christian and perhaps an escaped slave. No, Patrick would only cause trouble. He told Patrick to leave, and as Patrick walked away, he prayed.

Now that boat carried a cargo of hounds. They were good hunting dogs and worth a lot of money. The captain hoped to sell them in France. The dogs were nervous, and the crew was uneasy. They feared those savage dogs. But when Patrick came on board, he had calmed the dogs with ease. Now, as he left, the dogs began to snarl and whine.

Patrick's prayers were answered. The captain sent a man after him. "Come, hurry," he cried. "We shall take you on in good faith."

So Patrick sailed from Ireland. Joy filled his heart as he left that land behind.

The seas were smooth and calm. In three days, the ship reached France. War had made a desert of that part of the coast. The men traveled for many days, looking for people, food, and a place to sell their cargo. When they were so weary and weak from hunger that they could go on no longer, the captain went to Patrick. He said, "Tell me, Christian, you say that your God is great and all-powerful. Why, then, do you not pray for us? As you can see, we are suffering from hunger."

So Patrick prayed. He said that his God would send them food. That very day a herd of pigs crossed in front of them. The men killed many pigs. Both men and hounds ate their fill. For two days they stayed there. Then they moved on.

From that day on, Saint Patrick says, God gave them food, fire, and dry weather. Ten days later, they met people. They had traveled for 28 days.

Patrick left the traders after that time, and

we don't know for sure where he went. A scrap that has come down to us as a "Saying of Saint Patrick" states that he traveled through France, Italy, and the islands in the sea off Italy. Whatever he did during those years, the saying goes that the fear of God was his guide. If that saying is really Saint Patrick's, he may have tried to catch up on his schooling and learn more about God, for there were schools for monks in those places.

After a few years had passed, Patrick made his way back to Britain and his family. How happy they were to have him back! The long lost son had returned. They begged him to stay with them and never to leave them again.

God's Call

Patrick wanted to stay with his family in Britain very much. He had often thought about the time when he would be with them once again. Now that he was home, he planned to stay there.

Then one night he had a dream about a man coming to him from Ireland. The man carried many letters, and he gave one of them to Patrick. As Patrick began to read it, he saw the words, "The voice of the Irish." Then he heard voices calling from the woods, "We ask thee, boy, come and walk among us once more." Patrick woke up. What could the dream mean?

Another night he had a dream. Once more the voices called him. Then Patrick knew. He must go back to Ireland to take to them the Christian faith and give them hope. His God had work for him to do.

Patrick did not want to leave his home or family. Most of all, he did not want to go back to the place where he had been a slave. But Patrick loved the God he served. He cared for those who were not Christians. He thought that they must be brought to God. So he gave up all other plans and got ready to go.

Patrick went to France to learn to be a missionary. When he was ready, he sold his noble rank to raise money for his work. He bought the things he needed, had them all packed up, and hired a boat.

Many other people went with Patrick to Ireland. A bishop, a priest, and a chaplain went to help him preach. A cook went to make the meals. A brewer would make the drinks. Others came to serve the meals, drive the chariots, fix things, and do metal work. Women came to sew the cloths and linens for the churches. A guard was hired to protect Patrick from danger.

A cowherd came along to take care of the cows. Cows were used for trade. Each cow was worth an ounce of gold. In Ireland you could buy a servant girl for three cows or a servant boy for one cow!

A Baptism, a Barn, and a Death

Along the Irish shore there lived a man named Dichu. He was a chieftain and known as a good man. One fine day, as an old story goes, Dichu's servant came running to his master in great fear. As he was watching the pigs, he had seen an unknown boat pull up to shore. Strangely dressed men got out of the boat. "Raiders!" he thought, and tore off to tell Dichu.

Dichu called his hunting dog and picked up his sword and shield. He set off to stop the raiders. As he walked over his land, with his dog beside him, he saw a stranger walk up the hill. The dog ran ahead, snarling for a fight,

29

and then stopped, confused. The stranger had spoken softly and kindly. Was this man an enemy or a friend? Luckily, the dog must have decided that the strange man was a friend. He wagged his tail and licked Patrick's hand.

Dichu was surprised to see the change in his dog. He looked at Patrick closely. Patrick was a big, powerful man. He looked like a man of great strength. But when Dichu looked at Patrick's face, he saw only kindness and gentleness. He welcomed Patrick to his home.

Patrick stayed with Dichu and taught him about the Christian God. Dichu believed and had Patrick baptize him. Then he gave Patrick the barn that became Patrick's first church in Ireland.

For hundreds of years the Irish have sung a song to celebrate Dichu's gift:

God's blessing on Dichu
Who gave me the barn!
May he have afterwards
A heavenly home, bright, pure, great!

God's blessing on Dichu,
Dichu and all his children,
No child, grandchild or descendant of his
Shall die but after a long life.

A short time after he had come to Ireland, Patrick traveled north. He wanted to visit his old master, Miliucc. He wanted to give back the money Miliucc had paid to buy him so many years before. He also wanted to persuade Miliucc to accept the Christian faith.

Miliucc didn't want to see his former slave. When he heard that Patrick was coming, he shut himself up in his home. Then he gathered all his treasures around him and set it all on fire.

As Patrick came near, he saw the fire. He watched sadly as it burned. He said, "I know not, God knows. Yonder Miliucc's house is on fire. He is burning himself lest he believe in the Eternal God at the end of his life."

A New Faith

In Ireland at this time, almost 1600 years ago, there was an old, old religion that had been in France, too, before the Romans came. Very little is known about it, since its rites were kept secret by those who followed it. The leaders of this religion were called Druids. They were prophets, law givers, and teachers. Patrick had come to give the Irish a new religion. And it was no secret. Like other Christians then and now, Patrick saw himself as a bringer of Good News.

Patrick traveled tens of thousands of miles in his lifetime. He went to every part of Ireland.

Slowly he followed the rough tracks through the forests and bogs. Sometimes he used an ox-drawn cart. Sometimes he walked. Most of the time, though, he used his horses and chariots.

Everywhere he went, Patrick preached about God and His love. Many came to hear him. Many believed the things he told them. Patrick baptized them and had churches built for these new Christians. He quickly ran out of priests to help them and to run the churches. He had to train the Irish to do this work. His students included princes, Druids, writers, and poets. He taught them the Latin language and other things he thought they must know. As each year passed, the Catholic Church became stronger in Ireland.

Not everyone liked Patrick, nor did everyone want to follow this new religion. Patrick had many enemies. Some people feared and hated the man who had brought so much change to their country. One of them was the king of a place in Ireland called the Kingdom. He hated Patrick so much that he vowed to take Patrick's life. Odran,

Patrick's chariot driver, heard about the plot to kill him.

The next time Patrick returned to the Kingdom to preach, Odran asked him for a favor. "I have driven the chariot for a long time," he said. "Let me sit in your seat and rest, and you be the driver for a while."

Patrick gladly did as Odran had asked. As he drove through the Kingdom, the king threw his spear at the sitting man, thinking he was Patrick. Odran died instantly, but Patrick was able to escape. Odran had saved Patrick's life at the cost of his own.

Twelve times Patrick came close to losing his life. Once, Patrick tells us, he was put in prison. "They laid hands on me and my companions, and on that day they eagerly wished to kill me. . . . Everything they found with us they took away, and me they put in irons; and on the fourteenth day, the Lord delivered me from their power."

Patrick continued to preach until his death

on March 17, 461. He had been a man of great energy and drive. Others had a hard time trying to keep up with him. His body had been scarred from accidents and beatings. Through all, both bad and good, Patrick had a great love of God. And he taught the Irish to accept and love that same God.

In a short time churches were built all over Ireland. Church law became a living part of the law of the land. Boys and girls went to schools run by the church. Some of them became priests, monks, and nuns. Some of them, like Saint Patrick, brought the Christian faith to other lands. Irish monks built schools and monasteries in France, Germany, and Britain. Students of the church came to study in Ireland, too. No longer were the Irish cut off from the rest of the world.

Legends

Many stories have been told about Saint Patrick and the miracles he performed. Some of these things, such as the way God helped him to escape from slavery, Saint Patrick himself has told us about. Other stories have been handed down from parent to child for a thousand years and more, and now no one knows how they started. This is one of those legends that you may already know something about.

There are no snakes in Ireland, the Irish say, because Saint Patrick drove them out. He beat a drum so hard and so fast that the snakes couldn't stand the noise. They crawled out of

41

their hiding places and slithered into the sea.

All, that is, except for one big snake. It was an old snake, and maybe it was hard of hearing. Maybe it liked Patrick's funny music. Maybe it marched to a different drum. Whatever its reasons, this snake would not leave Ireland.

Already Patrick had played the drum so hard that he had made a hole in it. An angel had fixed the drum so that he could play on. Now his task was almost done except for this stubborn snake. If it wouldn't march to his drum like the others, something else would have to be done.

So Patrick put away the drum and built a box. He showed the box to the snake. "Look," he said, "I have made this box for you. It will make you a cozy home. Why don't you try it out?"

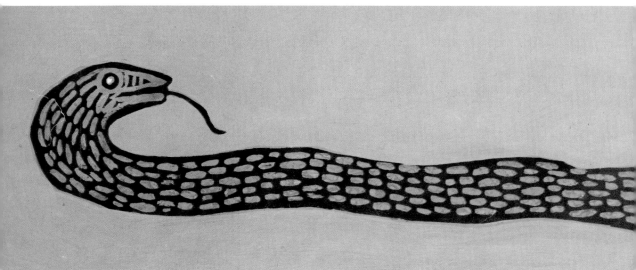

"No," the snake replied. "I don't want your box."

"Why not?" Patrick asked. "It's a nice box."

"It may be very nice," replied the snake, "but it's much too small for me."

"How do you know?" asked Patrick.

"Look at it," said the snake. "I'm much bigger than that box."

"No, I'm sure you can get into the box with ease," said Patrick.

"Don't be stupid," said the snake. He stretched himself out full length. "Look how long I am. I'll never fit in that box."

"Oh, it really is useless for us to argue about this," said Patrick. "Prove to me that you can't fit into the box."

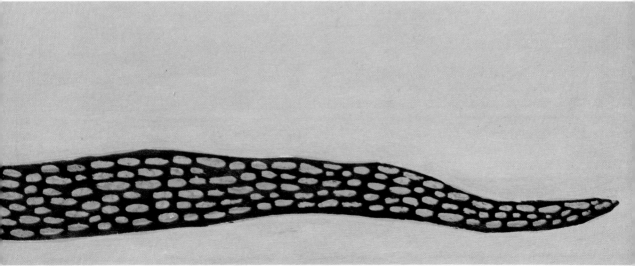

"No, I don't want to," replied the snake.

"Aha!" said Patrick, "that's because you know you will fit into the box."

"Okay," said the snake, "I'll show you."

The snake went to the box and entered it head first. "See?" said the snake. "Only a little bit of me fits in. The rest hangs out."

"Oh, come on," said Patrick. "How many times have I seen you curled up as you hid? If you curl up, I'm sure you'll fit into that box."

So the snake curled up and made himself as small as he could.

"See?" he said. "My head still sticks up above the box."

Patrick came near. "Pretend you're sleeping," he said, "and put your head down. Then all of you will be in the box."

"All right," said the snake, "but I'm telling you, this box will never be my home."

The snake bent his head down as if he were sleeping. Quickly Patrick slammed the lid and fastened it. Then he threw the box into the sea.

Since that time no poisonous snakes have ever been found in Ireland. Indeed, some people say that snakes die instantly upon touching Irish soil.

There are many other stories about Saint Patrick in Ireland. Now we have no way of knowing what's true and what the storytellers have added. What *is* true, though—what shines through every word—is the love and respect the Irish have for their very own saint.

Saint Patrick brings people together today as he did when he traveled to Ireland so many years ago. Today, thanks to the many, many Irish people who have come to live on our shores, there's a day in springtime when we'd all like to be just a little bit Irish. Happy Saint Patrick's Day!

About the Author

Saint Patrick, the Irish Saint is one of five children's books that Ruth Roquitte has written for Dillon Press. She is also the author of *A Day of Thanksgiving* and, with co-author Anne Stewart, of *Minnesota Adventures,* a three-unit state history series for upper elementary school students. A junior high school teacher and the mother of four children, Mrs. Roquitte lives in Morris, Minnesota. She received a baccalaureate in chemistry and physics from the University of Minnesota at Morris.

About the Illustrator

Robert Kilbride has illustrated several books, and his paintings are in the permanent collections of the Walker Art Center, the Minneapolis Institute of Arts, and the University Gallery of the University of Minnesota. He has also taught art at the University of Minnesota, the Walker Art Center, and the Minneapolis School of Art.

Mr. Kilbride was graduated from the Minneapolis School of Art and studied at the Académie de la Grande Chaumière in Paris. His works have been widely exhibited in the United States and France.